Dolphins

by Martha E. H. Rustad

Consulting Editor: Gail Saunders-Smith, Ph.D.

Consultant: Jody Byrum, Science Writer,
SeaWorld Education Department

Pebble Books

an imprint of Capstone Press
Mankato, Minnesota

Pebble Books are published by Capstone Press
151 Good Counsel Drive, P.O. Box 669, Mankato, Minnesota 56002
http://www.capstone-press.com

1 2 3 4 5 6 06 05 04 03 02 01

Library of Congress Cataloging-in-Publication Data
Rustad, Martha E. H. (Martha Elizabeth Hillman), 1975–
    Dolphins / by Martha E. H. Rustad.
    p. cm.—(Ocean life)
    Includes bibliographical references (p. 23) and index.
    ISBN 0-7368-0857-4
    1. Dolphins—Juvenile literature. [1. Dolphins.] I. Title. II. Series.
QL737.C432 R87 2001
599.53—dc21

00-009860

Summary: Simple text and photographs present dolphins and their behavior.

Note to Parents and Teachers

The Ocean Life series supports national science standards for units on the diversity and unity of life. The series shows that animals have features that help them live in different environments. This book describes dolphins and illustrates how they live. The photographs support early readers in understanding the text. The repetition of words and phrases helps early readers learn new words. This book also introduces early readers to subject-specific vocabulary words, which are defined in the Words to Know section. Early readers may need assistance to read some words and to use the Table of Contents, Words to Know, Read More, Internet Sites, and Index/Word List sections of the book.

Table of Contents

Dolphins are mammals.

blowhole

6

Dolphins breathe air
through a blowhole.

dorsal fin

Dolphins have
a dorsal fin.

flippers

10

Dolphins have
two flippers.

flukes

Dolphins have
two tail flukes.

Most dolphins live
in groups.

Dolphins communicate with each other.

Dolphins use echolocation to find food and objects.

Dolphins can jump.

Words to Know

blowhole—an opening on the top of a dolphin's head; a flap closes over the blowhole when the dolphin is underwater.

breathe—to take air in and out of the lungs; dolphins come to the water's surface to breathe through a blowhole.

communicate—to share information or feelings by making sounds or moving; dolphins squeak, whistle, click, and grunt.

dorsal fin—a part that sticks up on a dolphin's back; dorsal fins keep dolphins cool.

echolocation—using sound to find food and other objects; dolphins make sounds and listen for echoes that bounce off objects.

flipper—a flat limb with bones on a sea animal; flippers help dolphins balance and steer while they swim.

fluke—one of the two lobes of a dolphin's tail; flukes help dolphins swim.

mammal—a warm-blooded animal with a backbone; mammals feed milk to their young.

Read More

Berger, Melvin, and Gilda Berger. *Do Whales Have Belly Buttons?: Questions and Answers about Whales and Dolphins.* New York: Scholastic Reference, 1999.

Hodge, Judith. *Dolphins.* Animals of the Oceans. Hauppauge, N.Y.: Barron's Educational Series, 1997.

Richardson, Adele D. *Dolphins: Fins, Flippers, and Flukes.* The Wild World of Animals. Mankato, Minn.: Bridgestone Books, 2001.

Internet Sites

Bottlenose Dolphins
http://www.seaworld.org/bottlenose_dolphin/
bottlenose_dolphins.html

Bottlenose Dolphins
http://www.EnchantedLearning.com/subjects/whales/
species/Bottledolphin.shtml

Ultimate Guide: Dolphins
http://www.discovery.com/stories/nature/
dolphins/dolphins.html

Index/Word List

air, 7
blowhole, 7
breathe, 7
communicate, 17
dorsal fin, 9
each, 17
echolocation, 19
flippers, 11
food, 19

groups, 15
jump, 21
live, 15
mammals, 5
most, 15
objects, 19
other, 17
tail flukes, 13
two, 11, 13

Word Count: 44
Early-Intervention Level: 7

Credits
Steve Christensen, cover designer and illustrator; Kia Bielke, production designer;
    Kimberly Danger, photo researcher

Brandon D. Cole, 14
Corel Corporation, 16, 20
François Gohier, 8, 10
Mark Conlin and Mo Yung/www.norbertwu.com, cover
Melissa Martinez, 1
Norbert Wu/www.norbertwu.com, 4, 18
Norman Owen Tomalin/Bruce Coleman Inc., 6
Tom & Pat Leeson, 12